JOURNALS AND MORE

80157154R00066

Made in the USA
Las Vegas, NV
13 December 2020

TV show

NAME:
SEASONS:
EPISODES:

SEASON:

THE ENDING

-Thoughts-

Rating: ☆ ☆ ☆ ☆ ☆

TV
show

NAME:
SEASONS:
EPISODES:
SEASON:

THE ENDING

-Thoughts-

Rating: ☆ ☆ ☆ ☆ ☆

TV show

NAME:
SEASONS:
EPISODES:

SEASON:

THE ENDING

-Thoughts-

Rating: ☆ ☆ ☆ ☆ ☆

TV show

NAME:
SEASONS:
EPISODES:
SEASON:

<table>
<tr><td></td><td></td><td></td><td></td><td></td><td></td><td></td><td></td><td></td></tr>
<tr><td></td><td></td><td></td><td></td><td></td><td></td><td></td><td></td><td></td></tr>
</table>

THE ENDING

-Thoughts-

Rating: ☆ ☆ ☆ ☆ ☆

TV *show*

NAME:
SEASONS:
EPISODES:

SEASON:

THE ENDING

-Thoughts-

Rating: ☆ ☆ ☆ ☆ ☆

TV show

NAME:
SEASONS:
EPISODES:

SEASON:

THE ENDING

-Thoughts-

Rating: ☆ ☆ ☆ ☆ ☆

TV *show*

NAME:
SEASONS:
EPISODES:

SEASON:

THE ENDING

-Thoughts-

Rating: ☆ ☆ ☆ ☆ ☆

TV show

NAME:
SEASONS:
EPISODES:

SEASON:

THE ENDING

-Thoughts-

Rating: ☆ ☆ ☆ ☆ ☆

TV *show*

NAME:
SEASONS:
EPISODES:

SEASON:

THE ENDING

-Thoughts-

Rating: ☆ ☆ ☆ ☆ ☆

TV
show

NAME:
SEASONS:
EPISODES:

SEASON:

THE ENDING

-Thoughts-

Rating: ☆ ☆ ☆ ☆ ☆

TV *show*

NAME:
SEASONS:
EPISODES:

SEASON:

THE ENDING

-Thoughts-

Rating: ☆ ☆ ☆ ☆ ☆

TV show

NAME:
SEASONS:
EPISODES:
SEASON:

THE ENDING

-Thoughts-

Rating: ☆ ☆ ☆ ☆ ☆

TV *show*

NAME:
SEASONS:
EPISODES:

SEASON:

THE ENDING

-Thoughts-

Rating: ☆ ☆ ☆ ☆ ☆

TV show

NAME:
SEASONS:
EPISODES:
SEASON:

THE ENDING

-Thoughts-

Rating: ☆ ☆ ☆ ☆ ☆

TV *show*

NAME:
SEASONS:
EPISODES:

SEASON:

THE ENDING

-Thoughts-

Rating: ☆ ☆ ☆ ☆ ☆

TV *show*

NAME:
SEASONS:
EPISODES:
SEASON:

THE ENDING

-Thoughts-

Rating: ☆ ☆ ☆ ☆ ☆

TV show

NAME:
SEASONS:
EPISODES:

SEASON:

THE ENDING

-Thoughts-

Rating: ☆ ☆ ☆ ☆ ☆

TV show

NAME:
SEASONS:
EPISODES:

SEASON:

THE ENDING

-Thoughts-

Rating: ☆ ☆ ☆ ☆ ☆

TV show

NAME:
SEASONS:
EPISODES:

SEASON:

THE ENDING

-Thoughts-

Rating: ☆ ☆ ☆ ☆ ☆

TV *show*

NAME:
SEASONS:
EPISODES:

SEASON:

THE ENDING

-Thoughts-

Rating: ☆ ☆ ☆ ☆ ☆

TV *show*

NAME:
SEASONS:
EPISODES:

SEASON:

THE ENDING

-Thoughts-

Rating: ☆ ☆ ☆ ☆ ☆

TV show

NAME:
SEASONS:
EPISODES:

SEASON:

THE ENDING

-Thoughts-

Rating: ☆ ☆ ☆ ☆ ☆

TV *show*

NAME:
SEASONS:
EPISODES:

SEASON:

THE ENDING

-Thoughts-

Rating: ☆ ☆ ☆ ☆ ☆

TV *show*

NAME:
SEASONS:
EPISODES:

SEASON:

THE ENDING

-Thoughts-

Rating: ☆ ☆ ☆ ☆ ☆

TV
show

NAME:
SEASONS:
EPISODES:

SEASON:

THE ENDING

-Thoughts-

Rating: ☆ ☆ ☆ ☆ ☆

TV show

NAME:
SEASONS:
EPISODES:
SEASON:

THE ENDING

-Thoughts-

Rating: ☆ ☆ ☆ ☆ ☆

TV show

NAME:
SEASONS:
EPISODES:

SEASON:

THE ENDING

-Thoughts-

Rating: ☆ ☆ ☆ ☆ ☆

TV *show*

NAME:
SEASONS:
EPISODES:

SEASON:

THE ENDING

-Thoughts-

Rating: ☆ ☆ ☆ ☆ ☆

TV *show*

NAME:
SEASONS:
EPISODES:

SEASON:

THE ENDING

-Thoughts-

☆ ☆ ☆ ☆ ☆

Rating:

TV *show*

NAME:
SEASONS:
EPISODES:

SEASON:

THE ENDING

-Thoughts-

Rating: ☆ ☆ ☆ ☆ ☆

TV *show*

NAME:
SEASONS:
EPISODES:

SEASON:

THE ENDING

-Thoughts-

Rating: ☆ ☆ ☆ ☆ ☆

TV show

NAME:
SEASONS:
EPISODES:

SEASON:

THE ENDING

-Thoughts-

Rating: ☆ ☆ ☆ ☆ ☆

TV *show*

NAME:
SEASONS:
EPISODES:

SEASON:

THE ENDING

-Thoughts-

Rating: ☆ ☆ ☆ ☆ ☆

TV

show

NAME:
SEASONS:
EPISODES:
SEASON:

THE ENDING

-Thoughts-

Rating: ☆ ☆ ☆ ☆ ☆

TV *show*

NAME:
SEASONS:
EPISODES:

SEASON:

THE ENDING

-Thoughts-

Rating: ☆ ☆ ☆ ☆ ☆

TV *show*

NAME:
SEASONS:
EPISODES:

SEASON:

THE ENDING

-Thoughts-

Rating: ☆ ☆ ☆ ☆ ☆

TV *show*

NAME:
SEASONS:
EPISODES:

SEASON:

THE ENDING

-Thoughts-

Rating: ☆ ☆ ☆ ☆ ☆

TV
show

NAME:
SEASONS:
EPISODES:

SEASON:

THE ENDING

-Thoughts-

Rating: ☆ ☆ ☆ ☆ ☆

TV *show*

NAME:
SEASONS:
EPISODES:

SEASON:

THE ENDING

-Thoughts-

Rating: ☆ ☆ ☆ ☆ ☆

TV show

NAME:
SEASONS:
EPISODES:

SEASON:

THE ENDING

-Thoughts-

Rating: ☆ ☆ ☆ ☆ ☆

TV *show*

NAME:
SEASONS:
EPISODES:

SEASON:

THE ENDING

-Thoughts-

Rating: ☆ ☆ ☆ ☆ ☆

TV *show*

NAME:
SEASONS:
EPISODES:

SEASON:

THE ENDING

-Thoughts-

Rating: ☆ ☆ ☆ ☆ ☆

TV show

NAME:
SEASONS:
EPISODES:

SEASON:

THE ENDING

-Thoughts-

Rating: ☆ ☆ ☆ ☆ ☆

TV
show

NAME:
SEASONS:
EPISODES:

SEASON:

THE ENDING

-Thoughts-

Rating: ☆ ☆ ☆ ☆ ☆

TV shows

MUST WATCH!

- ◯
- ◯
- ◯
- ◯
- ◯
- ◯
- ◯
- ◯
- ◯
- ◯
- ◯
- ◯
- ◯

TV shows

MUST WATCH!

- ◯
- ◯
- ◯
- ◯
- ◯
- ◯
- ◯
- ◯
- ◯
- ◯
- ◯
- ◯
- ◯

TV shows

MUST WATCH!

- ◯
- ◯
- ◯
- ◯
- ◯
- ◯
- ◯
- ◯
- ◯
- ◯
- ◯
- ◯
- ◯

TV shows

MUST WATCH!

- ◯
- ◯
- ◯
- ◯
- ◯
- ◯
- ◯
- ◯
- ◯
- ◯
- ◯
- ◯
- ◯
- ◯

THIS

Tracker

BELONGS TO

_____